My Pc American Kitchen

Recipes with a Portuguese Accent

Easy and Delicious Recipes For the Home Cook

Author: Kevin M. Cordeiro

Copyright Year: © 2016
Language: English
Country: United States
All rights reserved. No part of this book may be reproduced, stored in a retrieval system or transmitted in any form, or be reproduced by any means, electronic, mechanical, photocopying, recording or otherwise without the prior written permission of the publisher, except by a reviewer who wishes to quote brief passages in connection with a review for magazine, broadcast, newspaper or internet.

Table of Contents

Introduction 5

How Portuguese Immigrants Came to New England 7

History 8

The Second Wave 12

Appetizers 13

    Grilled Sardines 15

    Fried Smelts 16

    Bacon Wrapped Chouriço Stuffed Dates 17

    Linguiça Cheese Swirls 18

    Bolinhos de Bacalhau (Cod Fish Balls) 19

    Fried Green Beans 20

    Portuguese Potato Skins 21

    Linguiça Clam Cakes 22

    Linguiça Cheese Bread Bowl 23

    Mini Meat Pies 24

    Salt Cod Puffs 25

    Camarão 'Pataniscas' (Shrimp Cakes) 26

    Linguiça Stuffed Mushrooms 27

    Stuffed Clams – "Quahog Stuffie" 28

Beef – Pork - Stews 29

    Madeira Beef Tips 31

    Portuguese Hash 32

    Crockpot Caçoila 33

    Brazilian Feijoada 34

    Portuguese Chop Suey 35

    Portuguese Braised Venison 36

    Portuguese Hot Stuff 37

    Marinated Pork Cutlets (Bifanas) 38

    Chouriço Bean Stew 39

- Portuguese Meat Pie 40
- Portuguese Spaghetti 41
- Portuguese Lasagna (No-Boil, Easy) 42
- Easy Portuguese Chili 43
- Chouriço Tamale Pie 44
- Portuguese Stuffed Cabbage Rolls 45
- Portuguese Stuffed Peppers 46

Chicken 47

- Chicken Madeira 49
- Roast Lemon Chicken 50
- Cranberry Chicken and Rice 51
- Hot and Spicy Fried Chicken 52
- Portuguese Grilled Chicken 53
- Piri Piri Grilled Chicken 54
- Roast Chicken with Potatoes and Chouriço 55
- Chicken Curry 56

Seafood 57

- Rhode Island Style Clams 59
- Bacalhau Casserole 60
- Bacalhau na Brasa 61
- Shrimp Mozambique 62
- Amêijoas 'à bulhão pato' 63
- Carne Porco à Alentejana 64
- Amêijoas à Espanhola 65
- Portuguese Mussels 66

Soup - Chowder - Sides 67

- Portuguese Kale Soup 69
- Shrimp Chouriço Corn Chowder 70
- Portuguese Clam Chowder 71
- Portuguese Rice 72

Sweets 73

Malasadas 75

Coconut Cupcakes (Bolinhos de Coco) 76

Pumpkin Dreams 77

Lemon Loaf 78

Coconut Cake (Bolo de Coco) 79

Pasteis de Nata (Custard Tarts) 80

Easy Apple Tart 82

Portuguese Rice Pudding (Arroz Doce) 83

Introduction

Lemon Loaf Recipe – page 78

Welcome to my kitchen, thank you for purchasing My Portuguese American Kitchen cookbook. It's filled with easy and delicious recipes. I love to cook and in case you didn't notice I'm Portuguese to the core. My blood bleeds red and green. But that doesn't mean I write off other cultures and their food. From the flavors of Italian cuisine to the corner Mexican or Asian market, I want to dive into it all and immerse myself.

I can walk down a street and see Thai food on my right, and a hamburger shop on my left. And only in America will these two get together to form Thai burgers! The possibilities are endless, and I draw inspiration from them. Don't get me wrong, I love my mother's Portuguese cooking, she's the best cook in the World. But when I can start with a Portuguese recipe and integrate something I might have tasted in an Asian restaurant; it takes it to another level. It's not about reinventing the wheel - just making it spin faster and more deliciously than it did before.

It's crazy to think that each state has anywhere from 10 to fifteen diverse cultures occupying it and bringing their food along for the ride.

Never underestimate this country and the people in it. I'm not the first person to say America is a "melting pot". All you have to do is make sure you keep the flame on low, stir it every now and then, and season to taste. You will get a new and exciting flavor every time you dip your spoon in.

I share traditional recipes and some Portuguese inflected recipes that I cook for family and friends, recipes with a Portuguese accent. I hope you love these recipes as much as I do and is a book that you will reach for again and again.

If you like this book, please take a moment to leave a review for this book. It really does make a difference.

If you want to keep you up to date for new recipes, cookbooks, and posts, follow me on Social Media.

Follow Kevin on Facebook: facebook.com/everydayportuguese
Twitter: twitter.com/kevinmarkc
Instagram: instagram.com/everydayportuguese
Pinterest: pinterest.com/everydayportuguese

Web Page: everydayportuguese.com

Thank you once again for your business.
Yours sincerely,
Kevin M. Cordeiro

How Portuguese Immigrants Came to New England

Celebrating the Feast of the Blessed Sacrament in the 1960s. Photo courtesy Museum of Madeiran History.

In 1915, four Madeiran men organized a feast at the Church of the Immaculate Conception in New Bedford, Mass., to celebrate the safe arrival of Portuguese immigrants after a stormy journey. The festival mimicked the traditional religious feast observed in their village on Madeira Island, with a celebration of the Roman Catholic Mass, a grand procession, traditional food, and folk dancing.

Today, the 100+ -year-old Feast of the Blessed Sacrament in New Bedford is the largest Portuguese festival in the world, reflecting both the size and the identity of the Portuguese-American population in New England.

Two great waves of Portuguese immigration gave Southeastern Massachusetts and Rhode Island the densest concentration of people with ancestry from Portugal, including the Azores and Cape Verde. They made their mark with restaurants and bakeries, with fishing fleets, and with Roman Catholic churches.

History

The first Portuguese sailor, Miguel Corte-Real, may have come to Massachusetts as far back as the early 16th century. A 40-ton boulder now in Dighton Rock State Park is inscribed with writing that Brown professor Edmund B. Delabarre believed were written by Corte-Real, in 1912, Delabarre wrote the inscriptions on the Dighton Rock said, "I, Miguel Cortereal, 1511. In this place, by the will of God, I became a chief of the Indians."

During the Colonial period, a small number of Portuguese immigrants came to the islands of Martha's Vineyard and Nantucket. Portuguese Jews immigrated early to America to escape persecution. Wealthy merchant Aaron Lopez and his associates brought the sperm oil industry to Newport, R.I., and built the Touro Synagogue in the 18th century.

Until about 1870, it was whaling that drew Portuguese sailors from the Azores and the Cape Verde Islands – and poverty and military service that sent them. They signed on for low-paying, dangerous work on whale ships and then settled in whaling communities in New England, California, and Hawaii. Portuguese families started to come to the United States in larger numbers around 1870 just as the whaling industry began to decline. They worked in New England's booming textile mills, in whaling and fishing. Women worked as seamstresses in garment shops.

In the late 19th century, many Portuguese, mainly Azorean and Madeiran, settled in Providence, Bristol and Pawtucket in Rhode Island, and New Bedford, Taunton, Fall River, Gloucester and Provincetown in Massachusetts. They also moved to Hartford and New Haven in Connecticut. "It was easy to get into this country in those early days," wrote Portuguese immigrant Lawrence Oliver in his autobiography. "America was a free port. To get in, all you needed was a little money in your pocket, so that the authorities could be sure you wouldn't be destitute and on relief right away."

Even during the Great Depression, Portuguese immigrants found opportunity in America. Capt. Joseph Captiva, a Provincetown fisherman, told a government interviewer in 1938.

In 1914, immigrants from Brava, Cape Verde, looking ashore from the Savoia as they await the disembarkation process to be finished. Photo courtesy New Bedford Standard-Times.

Evening recreation of the "Young Holy Ghosters" – Ages 15–25, average is 18 – all mill workers – all Portuguese. Location: Fall River, Massachusetts. Photograph by Lewis Wickes Hine, 21 June 1916. Photo courtesy Library of Congress.

The newcomers began to form fraternal benefit societies and to print their own newspapers, such as A civilizacao luso-americano in Boston. They maintained strong ties to the Roman Catholic Church and formed committees of festeiros to stage the religious festivals that survive today. The religious festivals helped Portuguese immigrants retain their sense of community and identity.

Throughout Massachusetts, Rhode Island and Connecticut, Portuguese religious festivals are held in the summer. They include- The Feast of the Blessed Sacrament in early August brings tens of thousands to New Bedford for folk dancing, pop music, soccer and traditional Madeiran food. The beverage of choice? Madeira wine, of course. The festival ends with a parade that follows a route marked by 70 arches of bayberry leaves, illuminated by twinkling lights.

The Feast of St. Anthony's in Pawtucket and Portsmouth, R.I., and Feast of the Holy Ghost in West Warwick, R.I.

The Festa do Divino Espirito Santo in East Taunton, Mass.

The Feast of the Holy Ghost in Fall River and the Provincetown Portuguese Festival and Blessing of the Fleet.

In Connecticut, a Portuguese Day Festival is held every year in Danbury and the Festa De Sao Joao is held in Waterbury. Portuguese residents of Stonington, Conn., hold an annual Feast of the Holy Ghost.

Portuguese immigration peaked between 1910 and 1920, then slowed considerably. Literacy was low in Portugal, and many Portuguese immigrants couldn't get in after the U.S. government instituted a literacy test in 1917. Then the government followed with a quota system that further reduced immigration from Portugal.

The Second Wave

A series of volcanic eruptions in the Azores from 1957-58 spurred the second wave of Portuguese immigration to the United States. The Capelinhos volcano, on the coast of the Azorean island of Faial, erupted on Sept. 27, 1957 and didn't stop until Oct. 24, 1958. No one was killed, but the volcanic activity covered the island with ash, destroyed homes and forced several thousand residents to leave. In September 1958, Congress passed the Azorean Refugee Act allowing 4,800 Azoreans to immigrate.

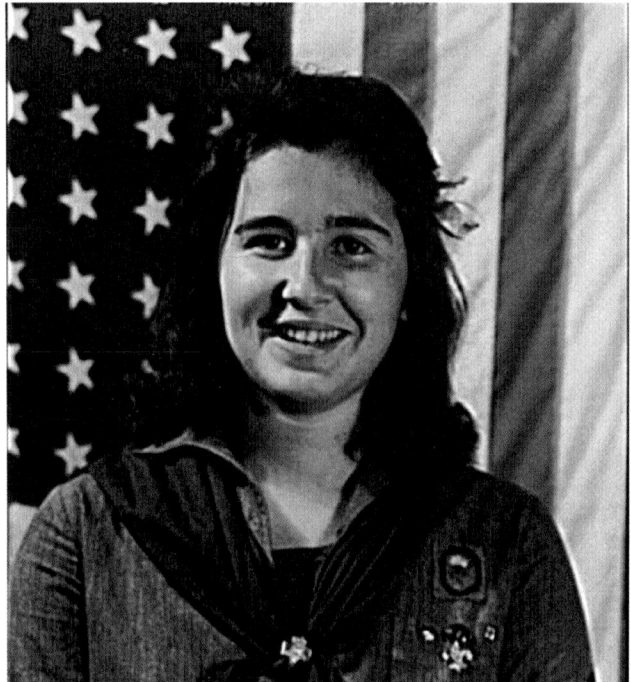

Portuguese-American Girl Scout, New Bedford, 1942. Photo courtesy Library of Congress.

Seven years later, the Immigration and Nationality Act of 1965 abolished the quota system and spurred a new wave of Portuguese immigration. Portuguese began to enter the United States at the rate of 11,000 to 12,000 per year. Between 1961 and 1990, 44.5 percent of all Portuguese immigration to the United States took place.

Portuguese immigrants make up only four-tenths of one percent (0.4 percent) of the entire U.S. population. In Rhode Island, Portuguese immigrants make up 9.7 percent of the population – the densest concentration of Portuguese in the country. Massachusetts ranks second, with 6.2 percent, Connecticut fourth, with 1.3 percent and New Hampshire with 1.2 percent.

The states with the largest Portuguese populations: Massachusetts: 379,722
California: 330,974 - Rhode Island: 99,445 - New Jersey: 78,196 - Florida: 48,974
Hawaii: 48,527 - per estimates of the 2010 Census.

Appetizers

Cod Fish Balls page 19

Grilled Sardines

Grilled the Portuguese way with olive oil and coarse salt, these sardines are delectable. Serve on thick slices of toasted bread that soften slightly and gain flavor as the sardine juices soak in. You'll be surprised how easy it is to fillet the sardines at the table; the meat virtually separates itself from the spine and bones.

Ingredients:
1-pound fresh sardines, cleaned, scaled, and gutted
3 medium garlic cloves, finely minced (about 1 tablespoon)
¼ cup extra virgin olive oil
¼ cup fresh juice from about 2 lemons
1 teaspoon paprika
½ teaspoon ground black pepper
Sea salt, or kosher salt
2 tablespoons chopped fresh parsley

Directions:
1. Combine the garlic, olive oil, lemon juice, paprika, and black pepper in a small bowl and whisk well to combine.
2. Arrange the sardines in a single layer on the bottom of a shallow baking dish and pour the marinade over the fish. Turn the fish to ensure they are coated evenly, and spoon some of the marinade into the cavity of each fish. Set aside to marinate for 30 minutes.
3. Pre-heat the grill. Alternatively, set all the burners on a gas grill to the highest heat setting, cover, and preheat for 10 minutes. Clean and oil the grilling grate.
4. Remove the sardines from the marinade and grill over direct heat until well-charred, 2 to 3 minutes. Using a metal spatula or grill fish turner, flip the sardines over and grill until charred on second side and cooked through, about 2 minutes longer.
5. Transfer the sardines to a large platter and season with salt.
6. Garnish with chopped parsley.

Fried Smelts

These small fish are very addictive. This simple recipe is easy, quick, and only 7 ingredients. Smelt is the name of a family of silvery fish found in cool waters. Most measure less than 8 inches (20 centimeters) long. Smelts have a small, fleshy fin behind the dorsal fin on the back like trout and salmon. This is very inexpensive, making it great for those on a tight budget.

Ingredients:
1-pound small smelt cleaned
1 cup flour
¼ cup cornstarch
2 teaspoons salt
¼ teaspoon garlic powder
¼ teaspoon ground black pepper
Peanut Oil

Directions:
1. With your hands, gently pry open the head of the fish and gently pull the gills along with the entrails. Rinse under cold running water and drain well. You can eliminate this step if you buy smelts already cleaned.
2. In a bowl, combine flour, cornstarch, salt, garlic powder and pepper. Dredge smelts in flour mixture to completely coat.
3. In a pot add about 2-inch deep of oil. Heat oil to 350 F.
4. Add fish, shaking off excess flour, and deep-fry for about 3 to 5 minutes or until golden and crisp.
5. Remove from heat and drain on paper towels.
6. Serve hot.

Bacon Wrapped Chouriço Stuffed Dates

Not only are these dates wrapped in bacon, they are also stuffed with chouriço. One bite and you're in sweet and spicy, bacon heaven! These dates are very easy to make. They are the perfect little bite to bring to a cookout or party. Party or not, you will want these. Bacon, chouriço and dates are wonderful together, simple, yet a fantastic appetizer. They will disappear, and your guests will be wanting more.

Ingredients:
1 link of chouriço, casing removed
24 dates pitted
12 slices of bacon cut in half

Directions:
1. Slice the chouriço into ¼ inch thick slices. Cut each slice into thirds, lengthwise. Each slice should give you 3 small rectangle pieces, close to the same shape of the date. Cut 24 pieces of rectangle pieces of chouriço.
2. Tuck one rectangle piece of chouriço into each date where the pit was removed. Pinch closed dates.
3. Wrap a strip of bacon around each date and secure with a toothpick.
4. Place the dates wrapped in a large frying pan, seam side down, and cook, turning, until the bacon is browned on all sides, about 10 minutes. You could also broil or grill. However, you normally cook your bacon should work just fine.
5. Drain and serve.

Linguiça Cheese Swirls

There is a delicious recipe on the back of the Pepperidge Farm Puff Pastry Sheet box for spinach cheese swirls. Here is my version with a Portuguese accent. They feature kale, linguiça, onion and cheese filling simply rolled up in flaky puff pastry and sliced into pinwheels. Makes 20 Swirls

Ingredients:
1 egg
1 tablespoon water
½ cup shredded pepper jack cheese
¼ cup grated Parmesan cheese
1 green onion chopped (about 2 tablespoons)
2 tablespoons all-purpose flour
½ pkg. of a 17.3-ounce package Pepperidge Farm Puff Pastry Sheets (1 sheet), thawed
1 cup ground linguiça
1 pkg. (about 10 ounces) frozen chopped kale, thawed and well drained

Directions:
1. Preheat the oven to 400°F.
2. In a pan, over medium high heat, sauté the linguiça and kale for 10 minutes. Set aside to cool.
3. Beat the egg and water in a small bowl and set aside.
4. Stir the pepper jack cheese, parmesan cheese, and onion in a medium bowl. Mix in the cooled linguiça and kale.
5. Sprinkle the flour on the work surface. Unfold the pastry sheet on the work surface. Brush the pastry sheet with the egg water mixture. Top with the cheese, linguiça, kale mixture.
6. Starting at a short side, roll up like a jelly roll. Cut into about 20 (1/2-inch) slices. Place the slices, cut-side down, onto 2 baking sheets. Brush the slices with the egg mixture.
7. Bake for 15 minutes or until the pastries are golden brown. Remove the pastries from the baking sheets and let cool for 10 minutes.

For best results, make sure to remove as much liquid as you can from the kale before adding to the sauté pan with the linguiça. If it's too wet, it may make the pastry soggy.

Bolinhos de Bacalhau (Cod Fish Balls)

Cod Fish Balls are probably the most popular appetizer in Portuguese cuisine. They are served at every party, gathering and celebrations. They are considered a must for Christmas and I remember my mom making them every New Year's Eve. Although it seems like a difficult process to prepare, they are relatively easy.

Ingredients:

½ pound boneless dried salt cod.
2 medium Russet or Idaho Potatoes peeled and cut into ½ inch slices
¼ teaspoon garlic powder
1 teaspoon dried parsley
1 large beaten egg
2 teaspoons olive oil
½ teaspoon black pepper
Vegetable oil for frying

Directions:
1. Place the salt cod in a large bowl with cold water and cover. Place in the refrigerator for 36 hours, changing the water every 12 hours.
2. Place the potatoes, and cod fish in a pan with enough water to cover. Cook on medium heat at a low boil for about 10 minutes. Gently remove the codfish which should be flaky and tender with a slotted spoon.
3. Place the codfish on a clean white linen kitchen towel or paper towels to absorb its moisture. Remove any pin bones.
4. After removing cod, continue cooking the potatoes for another 10 minutes or until fork tender and drain.
5. Roll the fish in the towel to form a ball and squeeze out any moisture. The drier the cod, the better.
6. When the potatoes are done drain and cool for about 10 minutes, once your cod and potatoes are cooled they will be ready to prep.
7. Flake the cod into tiny shreds with a fork until flaky and light but not mushy.
8. Mash the potatoes, then add the flaked cod, garlic, parsley, beaten egg, olive oil, and pepper to the potatoes and stir to incorporate the ingredients. Your batter should be thick enough to form into balls for frying. Shape them into 2 inch balls.
9. Heat your oil to about 370 degrees F. and begin frying 4 or five at a time for about 2 minutes until they are golden brown.
10. Test the first batch to be sure they are cooked in the middle. You may have to adjust the heat lower if you find they are turning brown too quickly and not cooking on the inside. Turn them over gently to cook each side.

Fried Green Beans

Peixinhos da horta is a traditional dish in Portuguese cuisine. The name of the dish is literally translated as "vegetable garden fishies", as it resembles small pieces of colorful fish. It was introduced to Japan by Portuguese-sponsored Jesuit missionaries in the sixteenth century. The Japanese loved the Portuguese idea of fried green beans they added other vegetables and eventually developed it into tempura.

Ingredients:
10 ½ ounces fresh green beans
1 cup all-purpose flour
3 eggs
¼ teaspoon ground black pepper
½ teaspoon dried parsley
½ teaspoon salt
Vegetable oil for frying

Directions:
1. Wash cut the ends and remove the green bean strings. Place them in a saucepan with water seasoned with salt. Bring to a boil over high heat.
2. When water starts boiling, reduce to low heat, and cook about 15 to 20 minutes. When the green beans are cooked, drain them well and set aside.
3. Place the flour, eggs, pepper, parsley, and salt in a bowl and stir with a fork until you have a creamy mixture.
4. Dip each green bean in the eggs/flour mixture.
5. Heat the oil in a skillet. When the oil is hot, add the green beans and fry on both sides until golden brown.
6. When they are fried, place them on a plate with paper towel.

Portuguese Potato Skins

If there is one snack or appetizer that I always like to order at a restaurant or see at a football tailgate, its potato skins. Here is an American favorite with a Portuguese accent. These potato skins are a crispy tasty delight. Stuffed with linguiça and cheese, it makes an easy hot appetizer to enjoy right out of the oven or at room temperature. Serves 6

Ingredients:
4 medium russet potatoes
1 tablespoon snipped fresh chives
¼ cup butter, melted
1 ½ cups shredded cheddar cheese
½ cup ground linguiça

Directions:
1. Poke potatoes with a fork on both sides. This will prevent them from bursting in microwave.
2. Microwave potatoes for 6 minutes. Turn over potatoes and microwave for another 6 minutes. Cook a little longer if potatoes are not fully cooked. Potatoes should be soft.
3. When the potatoes are cool enough to handle, make 2 lengthwise cuts through each potato. Resulting in three 1/2-inch slices per potato (the 2 skin ends and the middle). Discard the middle slice or save them for a separate dish of mashed potatoes. This will leave you with two potato skins per potato (see image)
4. With a spoon, scoop some of the potato out of each skin, being sure to leave about ¼ inch of potato inside of the skin.
5. Brush the entire surface of each potato skin, inside and outside, with the melted butter.
6. Place the skins on a cookie sheet, cut side up, and broil them for 6 to 8 minutes or until the edges begin to turn dark brown.
7. Sprinkle 2 to 3 tablespoons of Cheddar cheese into each skin.
8. Sprinkle the ground linguiça onto the cheese.
9. Broil the skins for 2 more minutes or until the cheese is thoroughly melted. Serve hot

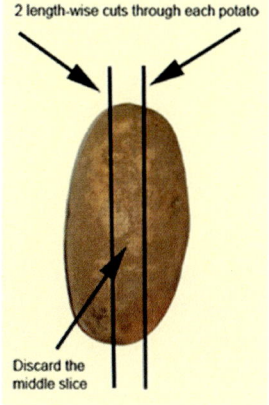

Linguiça Clam Cakes

What is summer without linguiça clam cakes. Something you might have never heard of, but frankly, irresistible—as a kid, I remember getting clam cakes at Lincoln Park in North Dartmouth, MA. Such a great New England treat. But now with linguiça in it? The crispy pieces on linguiça on the edges of the clam cakes are irresistible!
Make about 14 cakes

Dry Ingredients:
2 cups flour
1 teaspoons baking powder
¼ teaspoon onion powder
1 ½ teaspoons salt
¼ teaspoon black pepper
1 teaspoon sugar

Wet Ingredients:
1 egg
¾ cup claim juice
¼ cup milk
8 oz. (½ pound) of chopped clams, drained
⅓ cup ground linguiça or chouriço (optional)
It is not necessary to cook the linguiça or chouriço before adding to batter.

Directions:
1. Mix together the dry ingredients and set aside.
2. In a medium bowl mix the egg, clam juice, and milk.
3. Add dry ingredients to the wet ingredients, a little at a time, stirring well until the mixture is sticky.
4. Mix in clams and linguiça or chouriço.
5. Drop by tablespoon into medium hot oil in a deep fryer or heavy skillet.
6. A good starting temperature is 375 degrees.
7. The clam cakes will float; turn them over gently as they rise to fully cook both sides. Do not overload the cooker, as this will reduce heat too much.
8. Drain on paper towels. These are best while still warm but can be served at room temperature as well.

Linguiça Cheese Bread Bowl

Crumbles ground linguiça and cheddar cheese into a crispy bread bowl for a warm and savory treat that is great for any occasion. A simple and delicious recipe that's easy to make and always a hit. Best part about it is you can eat the bowl. Serves 2

Ingredients:
2 mini French boules or 2 large crusty hard rolls
¼ cup of ground linguiça
1 can of Campbell's cheddar cheese condensed soup
¼ cup milk
2 teaspoons of mayonnaise
¼ teaspoon dried parsley
½ cup mozzarella cheese
¼ of an onion
1 pinch of cayenne pepper

Directions:
1. Preheat oven to 425 F.
2. Cut the tops of the rolls. Empty the inside of bread bowl and toast the tops (cover for the bread bowl)
3. In a blender or food processor, blend the soup, milk and onion, blend well until a puree texture.
4. Add this mixture to a sauce pan and bring to a simmer.
5. Add the linguiça, mayonnaise, parsley, salt and pepper.
6. Cook for 10 minutes stirring often so not to stick to pan.
7. Remove from heat and pour into bread bowls
8. Add ¼ cup of mozzarella cheese on top of each bread bowl on the soup.
9. Bake for about 15 minutes or until the cheese is bubbly.
10. Remove from oven and serve immediately with the toasted top to cover.

Mini Meat Pies

Beef pot pie just got a tasty makeover with chouriço! Made in muffin tins, easy to make and they taste incredible. Golden crisp pastry on the outside, delicious succulent meat on the inside.
Makes 12 mini pies

Ingredients:

½ pound ground beef
½ pound ground chouriço
½ teaspoon salt
1 tablespoon minced garlic
¼ teaspoon ground black pepper
3 tablespoons olive oil
1 medium onion diced
2 medium ripe tomatoes peeled and diced
½ teaspoon dried parsley
1 egg yolk
2 boxes frozen Pepperidge Farm Puff Pastry Sheets
2 muffin pans (6-hole large-size muffin pan)

Directions:
1. Add ground meats to a bowl and season the meat with salt, garlic, and pepper. Mix the spices in the meat and set aside.
2. In a saucepan heat olive oil over medium heat. Add onion and the tomatoes. Sauté until the tomato starts to break down.
3. Add the meat with spices, stir and cook about 10 to 15 minutes. Stir occasionally.
4. Turn off the heat and sprinkle with parsley.
5. Grease 2 (6-hole large-size muffin pans). Extend the puff pastry on a lightly floured surface, cut out circles from a sheets of puff pastry and use them to line the base and sides of muffin tins.
6. Fill with the meat and cover with a small circle of dough. Press slightly the edges with your fingers to seal the top with the sides of the dough.
7. Brush on top with beaten egg yolk.
8. Pre-heat oven to 350° F.
9. Bake 15 to 20 minutes.
10. Remove pies from the oven, cool 10 minutes.
11. Remove mini pies from pan and serve.

Salt Cod Puffs

These puffs are just so good, quick, and easy to make. It just has everything going for it, salted cod sautéed in olive oil, onion, and garlic, mixed with chopped hard-boiled eggs and Alfredo sauce. You can pair this appetizer with a white wine like, Pinot Grigio or a Portuguese wine like Arinto or the crisp flavor of Loureiro. Makes 24 puffs

Ingredients:

10 ½ ounces salt cod
3 tablespoons olive oil
1 medium onion
3 teaspoons minced garlic
¼ teaspoon ground black pepper
⅛ teaspoon dry ground nutmeg
A pinch salt
2 egg yolk
2 whole hard-boiled eggs, peeled
½ cup of Prego Alfredo sauce
1 box frozen Pepperidge Farm Puff Pastry Sheets

Directions:

1. Place the salt cod in a large bowl with cold water and cover. Place in the refrigerator for 36 hours, changing the water every 12 hours.
2. Heat a pan with water. Place the desalted cod and simmer about ten minutes. When the cod is cooked, place it on a plate, remove any skins and spines. Place the codfish on a clean white linen kitchen towel or paper towels to absorb its moisture then shred it into slivers. Set aside.
3. Place the olive oil in a pan and heat over medium high heat, along with the chopped onion and the minced garlic. Sauté about five minutes.
4. Add the shredded cod, season with pepper, nutmeg, and pinch of salt, stir and cook about five minutes. Turn off the heat, add the chopped hard-boiled eggs and Alfredo sauce, mix everything well.
5. Extend one of the puff pastries on a table sprinkled with flour. Cut out 12 squares from pastry sheet. Repeat with the second pastry sheet.
6. Place on each one of them a small portion of the cod filling. Brush the edges with the beaten egg yolks and close them over the filling giving them the shape of a rectangle. Press rectangle edge together and tuck under a little.
7. Brush the top of each one with the remaining egg yolk.
8. Preheat oven at 350° F.
9. Bake about 20 to 25 minutes until golden.

Camarão 'Pataniscas' (Shrimp Cakes)

Shrimp creates a pleasing variation to crab cakes. These spicy shrimp cakes are a delicious way to cook shrimp. Looking to add more shellfish to your diet, try this delicious shrimp recipe. This recipe includes a jalapeno pepper to add a little kick--very flavorful! You can't go wrong paired with a dry white wine like Chablis or Portuguese extra dry wine like Fonseca Siroco.

Ingredients:
1 (4oz.) can tiny shrimp
2 eggs, beaten
1 cup plus 2 tablespoons flour
⅓ cup water
1 jalapeno pepper diced (remove seeds and veins)
½ teaspoon dried parsley
¼ teaspoon dried coriander
1 green onion stalk diced
1 teaspoon minced garlic
1 teaspoon baking powder
1 teaspoon salt
¼ teaspoon ground black pepper
Vegetable oil for frying

Directions:
1. In a large bowl, combine the eggs, flour with 6 tablespoons water.
2. Then, add the jalapeno pepper, parsley, coriander, shrimp, onion, garlic, baking powder, salt and pepper.
3. Mix thoroughly until blended (add more water if you find that the dough is too thick or more flour if you think that is too liquid.
4. Heat the oil over medium high heat in a skillet. When the oil is hot, remove small portions of the mixture with a spoon and fry them on both sides until golden. (while frying, flatten).
5. When they are fried, place them on a plate with paper towels.
6. Serve and Enjoy!

Linguiça Stuffed Mushrooms

With potlucks, open houses, and holiday gatherings, it doesn't hurt to have a signature dish. Linguiça Stuffed mushrooms are a crowd favorite, so if you don't already have a recipe stashed away, I promise this one will become a greatest hit! This recipe is simple on assembly but big on flavor. There are a million and one versions of stuffed mushrooms out there, but this is the one that I consider to be my favorite.

Ingredients:
24 whole mushrooms
2 tablespoons butter
1 tablespoon olive oil
½ cup of ground Linguiça
1 - 6 oz. can crab meat, drained
¼ teaspoon garlic powder
¼ teaspoon ground black pepper
¼ cup grated Parmesan cheese
¼ cup Italian blend shredded cheese
¼ cup Italian style dry bread crumbs
½ cup white wine

Directions:
1. Twist mushroom stems to remove from mushroom caps. Finely chop enough stems to measure 1 cup. Set aside mushroom caps.
2. Heat butter and olive oil in a medium saucepan over medium heat. Stir in the chopped stems and linguiça. Sauté for 10 minutes and remove from heat.
3. Mix in, the crab meat, garlic powder, black pepper, Parmesan cheese, shredded cheese, and dry bread crumbs.
4. Fill the mushroom caps. Use the palm of your hand to press and overstuff mushrooms.
5. Add wine to a 13"x9" baking dish. Add stuffed mushrooms to the dish.
6. Bake at 375° F. for 25 minutes.

Stuffed Clams – "Quahog Stuffie"

Quahog is a type of large hard-shell clam, which is used in this popular baked stuffed quahog recipe. This was by far the best-selling item in my days of catering. Everyone loved them! Every cook and household have their own take on how to make stuffed quahogs. It can be mild or spicy, depending on your preference. I love theses with some spicy heat from the chouriço sausage and jalapeno pepper. Makes 12 stuffies

Ingredients:

12 Large quahogs
3 tablespoons olive oil
3 tablespoons butter
½ pound ground chouriço
1 large onions
1 small red bell pepper diced (remove seeds and veins)
1 jalapeno pepper diced (remove seeds and veins)
½ teaspoon white pepper
½ teaspoons salt
1 tablespoon minced garlic
½ cup clam juice
1 cup water
18 slices fresh white bread, crusts removed (Pulse bread in a food processor until coarse bread crumb consistency)
1 cup plan dry breadcrumb

Directions:
1. Shuck* quahogs raw, rinse and cut up to bite size pieces, set aside.
2. In a large skillet, heat oil and butter over medium high heat.
3. Add onions, diced peppers and chouriço. Reduce heat and simmer for about 15 minutes.
4. In a large bowl add cooked onions, peppers and chouriço. Then add quahog meat, white pepper, salt, garlic, clam juice and water. Mix well.
5. Slowly mix in slices of crumbled fresh bread. Stir till well blended and the bread is absorbed.
6. Mix in dry breadcrumbs. Mix till all the crumbs are absorbed.
7. Let stuffing rest for about 10 minutes. You can also cover and refrigerate and stuff shells at a later time.
8. Stuff 12 shells piled high, sprinkle top with paprika.
9. Bake in 400 degrees F. Cook for 30 minutes.

*You can quickly steam the clams till they start too open to make it easier to shuck them or put the clams in your freezer 30 minutes to shucking and that makes it much easier too.

Beef – Pork - Stews

Chouriço Stew page 39

Madeira Beef Tips

This Portuguese dish originates from the island of Madeira. It involves simple ingredients but delivers amazing flavors. The beef is tender and melts in your mouth.

Ingredients:
1 pound of stew beef cubed
1 onion sliced
1 ½ cup beef broth
1 tablespoon olive oil
1 tablespoon butter

Marinade:
2 tablespoon Kocher salt
2 bay leaves each cut in half
½ teaspoon dry hot crushed red pepper
1 teaspoon garlic powder
½ teaspoon ground black pepper
1 cup Madeira wine

Directions:
1. Marinate beef in fridge for 12 -24 hours.
2. Heat olive oil in pan and add beef. Braise over medium high heat. When meat is browned add to crockpot.
3. When all the beef is browned, add beef broth to the hot pan to deglaze. Then add all these tasty drippings from the pan to the crock pot with the meat.
4. Mix in onions and add butter to the crock pot.
5. Cover crockpot cook for 2 hours on hi or 4 hours on low.

Portuguese Hash

Hash is most well known in its corned beef iteration, complete with a couple of fried eggs on top. It doesn't have to involve corned beef. And honestly, the eggs are optional, too. This hash recipe has chouriço and you'll find yourself making it for breakfast, lunch, dinner, and whenever else you happen to have a craving. Perfectly cooked potatoes paired with the flavors of chouriço make this Portuguese Hash truly unforgettable!

Ingredients:
1-pound ground beef
1 link of chouriço, diced
2 large potatoes peeled and diced
1 teaspoon salt
½ teaspoon paprika
½ teaspoon ground black pepper
¼ teaspoon garlic powder
1 tablespoon butter
1 tablespoon olive oil
½ cup water
2 tablespoons ketchup

Directions:
1. In a large pan, brown ground beef and drain.
2. Mix in chouriço, potatoes, salt, paprika, pepper, garlic, butter, oil and water.
3. Cover and simmer for 15 minutes.
4. Mix in ketchup, cover, and cook an additional 5 minutes or until potatoes are cooked.

Crockpot Caçoila

Caçoila is a delicious Portuguese-style of pulled pork or beef. There are countless versions of caçoila [ka-soy-la, although some folks say ka-sir-la] using different types of meat, such as pork, beef and liver, and different ways of serving it, like in a bowl or as a sandwich. Some add vinegar and cinnamon instead of wine and allspice. Recipes vary from family to family and region to region, whether in the United States, Azores, Madeira, Cape Verde, Brazil or in Portugal, they all have one thing in common, a long cooking process to ensure meat is very tender. What I am sharing, reflect my Portuguese heritage. This is one of my food loves. I am addicted to this delectable slow-roasted meat and spices. This sandwich is very simple, meat and bread, but the flavor is so incredible! If you try this, you will understand why this savory, aromatic, salty, tender, juicy, slow-cooked meat ranks as one of my personal favorite dishes. A mixture of pork or both pork and beef can be used. Serves 8

Ingredients:
2 tablespoons olive oil
1-pound boneless pork cut into cube pieces.
1-pound boneless beef cut into cube pieces.
1 link of chouriço, casing removed, cut into cubes (optional)
2 medium onions (chopped)
2 teaspoons minced garlic
1 ½ teaspoons salt
1 teaspoon paprika
½ teaspoon ground black pepper
1 teaspoon allspice
½ teaspoon crushed red hot pepper flakes
1 bay leaf
1 (8 oz.) can tomato sauce.
½ cup red wine (red port wine is good)

Directions:
1. Mix all ingredients together in crock-pot.
2. Cover and cook for 4 hours on high or 8 hours on low.
3. Remove bay leaf.
4. Break meat apart and mix. Meat will at first have a lot of liquid, but as you mash and break meat apart and mix in, it will get to a pulled pork consistency.

Brazilian Feijoada

A rich black bean stew with pork, beef and chouriço. Feijoada (pronounced fay-ZWAH-da) is a delicious stew that's traditionally served with rice. In Brazil, this dish is often served on special occasions, but preparing it in a slow cooker makes it possible to serve this rich dish on the busiest weeknights. Serves 6

Ingredients:
1 large onion diced
½ pound bacon diced
1 link of chouriço, sliced
1 pound of beef for stew
1 pound of boneless pork cutlets cut into cubes
1 tablespoon of crushed garlic
1 beef bouillon cube
1 teaspoon salt
½ teaspoon ground coriander
½ teaspoon black pepper
1 bay leaf
1 cup white wine
2 cans black beans with their juices
Orange washed and cut into slices for garnish

Directions:
1. Mix in all above ingredients to a crockpot except black beans.
2. Cover and cook on high for 3 hours or 6 hours on low.
3. Add beans and mix in. Cook on high for an additional hour.
4. Remove bay leaf and serve.

Serve with white rice.

Portuguese Chop Suey

A delicious American classic made with chouriço. This is a great comfort food. Left overs can be frozen and make another meal or quick lunch. Serve with some crusty bread or garlic bread.
Serves 4

Ingredients:
1 large onion chopped
½ of a green pepper, chopped
1 pound of ground chouriço
¼ cup ketchup
1 cup tomato sauce
½ teaspoons salt
½ teaspoon black pepper
½ teaspoon crushed hot red pepper flakes
1 cup hot water
½ cup grated parmesan cheese
½ pound of elbow macaroni

Directions:
1. Cook elbow macaroni per package directions. Drain and toss with a little oil to keep it moist. Set aside.
2. Add oil to a large saucepan and heat on medium high heat.
3. Add onion and green pepper. Sauté for 10 minutes.
4. Add chouriço to pan. Cook for 10 minutes.
5. Add the water, ketchup, tomato sauce, salt, black pepper and hot pepper. Mix everything together.
6. Simmer and cook for 20 minutes, stir occasionally.
7. Add cooked macaroni and mix well, cook for 10 minutes, stirring occasionally.
8. Remove from stove and mix in parmesan cheese.

Portuguese Braised Venison

Venison shoulder is the perfect cut for this dish because it's lean and tough. The tasty muscles respond perfectly to slow cooking. If you have difficulty finding a shoulder, use venison shanks instead. Serves 4

Ingredients:
2 pounds cubed shoulder of venison
1 link of chouriço, sliced
½ pound thick cut bacon, cut into 1-inch pieces
2 tablespoons olive oil
1 package of button mushrooms
2 sprigs fresh thyme
2 bay leaves
1 teaspoon paprika
1 teaspoon salt
½ teaspoon ground black pepper
2 medium onions sliced
2 teaspoons minced garlic
1 cup of Madeira wine
1 cup of beef broth

Directions:
1. Begin by heating the oil in a sauté pan over medium high heat, when it's hot, add the bacon and venison to the pan.
2. Cook bacon and brown the cubes of venison, about 6 at a time, removing them and adding them to the crock pot as the meat browns on all sides.
3. Once bacon and all the meat has been browned add the bacon and the pan drippings to the crock pot.
4. Add the sliced chouriço, fresh mushrooms, 1 of the sprigs of fresh thyme, bay leaves, paprika, salt, pepper, onions, garlic, wine and beef broth to your crock pot.
5. Mix everything together.
6. Cover with lid and cook 4 hours on high or 8 hours on low.
7. Transfer the venison to a serving dish and garnish with sprig of fresh thyme.

Portuguese Hot Stuff

A mainstay of Rhode Island. Known as dynamites or a torpedo. It's a specific kind of sandwich, eaten on a roll. That may sound like a Sloppy Joe, but whatever you call it, it's one tasty sandwich. Kicked up a notch with Portuguese hotness. Chouriço and 3 hot peppers make this a 3 Alarm hot and spicy sandwich that will keep you coming back for more. Can you handle the heat! So Delicious! Cooks right in your crock pot. Serves 6

Ingredients:
1-pound ground beef
1-pound ground chouriço
1 large green pepper chopped
1 jalapeno pepper (remove the seeds and inside white veins)
1 large onion chopped
1 (8) oz. can tomato sauce
1 (15) oz. can diced tomatoes, liquid and all.
½ tablespoon tomato paste mixed in ¼ cup of water
1 teaspoon paprika
½ teaspoon crushed red hot pepper flakes
¼ teaspoon Cayenne pepper
2 teaspoons salt
½ teaspoon black pepper

Directions:
1. Brown ground beef and drain to remove grease. No need to brown chouriço.
2. Add beef and all other ingredients to Crock Pot, mix well.
3. Cover and cook on high for 4 hours, stirring occasionally.
4. Serve on your favorite roll.

Marinated Pork Cutlets (Bifanas)

The Portuguese people eat these pork sandwiches like we Americans eat burgers -- anytime and anywhere. The Bifana is so popular, McDonald's even launched the McBifana in Portugal. The Alentejo region is said to be where the bifana originated, in the town of Vendas Novas. Most locals will tell you that the best bifanas are from this area, and supposedly they are a cut above those made elsewhere. It is a perfect storm of flavors and textures coming together to sweep you up and take your taste buds to wanting more and more. This recipe is from the Alentejo region of Portugal. Makes 4 sandwiches.

Ingredients:
Boneless pork thinly sliced about a ¼ inch thick (8 slices)
1 cup beef broth
2 tablespoons of olive oil

Marinade:
1 cup red port wine
2 tablespoons red wine vinegar
2 tablespoon Kocher salt
½ teaspoon ground black pepper
1 ½ teaspoons garlic powder
½ teaspoon onion powder

1 teaspoon sugar
1 tablespoon paprika
½ teaspoon dried crushed hot red pepper
½ teaspoon allspice
2 bay leaves, broken in half

Directions:
1. Marinate pork for 12-24 hours.
2. In a large skillet, heat 2 tablespoons of olive oil over medium-high heat.
3. Remove 4 cutlets from the marinade, add them to the heated skillet. Sauté until just beginning to brown on both sides, turning only once, about 1 ½ minutes per side. Do not overcook.
4. Remove pork from skillet and transfer to a serving plate. Repeat this process with remaining 4 cutlets.
5. Once all the cutlets are sautéed, add 1 cup of beef broth to the hot drippings in the pan. Stirring constantly, cook until mixture is thickened, about 45-60 seconds. Remove from heat.
6. Drizzle the pan dripping over the cutlets.
7. Assemble four beautiful bifana sandwiches. Two cutlets per sandwich.

Chouriço Bean Stew

Spice up your stew with chouriço and stir in some beans for a super dinner. High flavor fills each bowl of this bean stew thanks to the chouriço. This Portuguese-influenced stew is chockful of flavors, making it a perfect one-dish meal. Slow cooked right in your crock-pot.

Ingredients:
1 large red bell pepper sliced
2 onions finely chopped
2 links of chouriço, sliced
1 teaspoon paprika
1 tablespoon minced garlic
½ cup beer
2 cups crushed tomatoes, ground peeled
1 can of chickpeas, drained
1 can cannellini beans, drained
½ teaspoon salt
¼ teaspoon ground black pepper
Parsley, to garnish

Directions:
1. Add all ingredients to Crock Pot, mix well.
2. Cover and cook on high for 3 hours or low for 6 hours, stirring occasionally.

Portuguese Meat Pie

You may have tried a French meat pie made with beef, pork, and potato, nicely spiced and baked into a pie crust. I must say, this is a delicious recipe where the French and Portuguese get together to form a tasty meat pie that takes it to another level. The results are overwhelming. You will not be able to stop at just one slice. Enjoy! Serves 8

Ingredients:

1 package Pillsbury Just Unroll Pie Crusts
1 cup dry seasoned bread crumbs
1-pound ground pork
1-pound ground chouriço or linguiça
1 cup potatoes peeled and diced
1 onion diced
½ cup dry red wine (like port wine)
¼ cup water
¼ cup ketchup
½ cup to tomato sauce
2 teaspoons minced garlic
1 ½ teaspoons salt
½ teaspoon ground black pepper
½ teaspoon hot crushed red pepper flakes
1 teaspoon parsley
1 teaspoon paprika

Directions:

1. Add all ingredients, EXCEPT pie crust and bread crumbs, to a large pan and bring to a boil.
2. Cover and reduce heat and simmer for 30 minutes.
3. When cooked, mash everything in the pan together with a masher.
4. Mix in Bread crumb.
5. Pre-heat oven to 400 F.
6. Unroll 1 pie crust to a greased pie dish
7. Spoon in filling, spreading evenly.
8. Unroll second pie crust and cover on top of filling and pinch edges to seal. Cut slits in top crust so steam can escape.
9. Cover around edges of pie dish with strips of aluminum foil, bake 30 minutes.
10. Remove foil and bake another 30 minutes.

Portuguese Spaghetti

I bet you envision a spaghetti dish full of tomato sauce. This dish is light on the tomato sauce with, ground beef and chouriço. This recipe is where the Italian, Asian and Portuguese get together to form the best spaghetti dish ever. An exceptional tasting dish.
Serves 8

Ingredients:
2 large onions sliced and cut into quarters
2 tablespoons of olive oil
2 tablespoons minced garlic
1-pound ground beef
1-pound ground chouriço
1 teaspoon salt
½ teaspoon black pepper
1 28oz can crushed tomatoes, ground peeled (Chunky Style)
¼ cup soy sauce
½ teaspoon dry basil
1-pound spaghetti cooked in water

Directions:
1. Cook pasta per package directions. Drain and toss with a little oil to keep it moist. Set aside.
2. In a large skillet, over medium-high heat add olive oil and sauté onions and garlic until translucent, about 10 minutes.
3. Add the ground meats, salt and pepper and sauté until browned, about 10 minutes.
4. Add the crushed tomato, soy sauce and basil and bring to a simmer.
5. Simmer for an hour stirring occasionally.
6. Combine spaghetti with sauce in pasta pot and serve.

Left overs can be frozen and make another meal or quick lunch.

Portuguese Lasagna (No-Boil, Easy)

I'm sure everyone has their own favorite lasagna recipe, but I'd just like to offer that this is the Best Lasagna Ever. This recipe gets its Portuguese accent with ground chouriço instead of ground beef. By adding red wine, to the sauce you get a bolder richer flavor. This recipe is a delicious pairing of Italian and Portuguese influences.

Ingredients:
2-pound ground chouriço
1 (28) oz. jar of your favorite pasta sauce
1 (15) oz. can diced tomatoes, with liquid
1 cup water

½ cup red wine
1 teaspoon crushed garlic
1 teaspoon salt
½ teaspoon ground black pepper
1 green bell pepper finely chopped
1 red bell pepper finely chopped
1 yellow pepper finely chopped
½ cup grated parmesan cheese
3 cups shredded mozzarella cheese
1 (8 ounce) packages no-boil lasagna noodles

Directions:
1. Pre-heat oven to 350 degrees F.
2. In large pan add chouriço, pasta sauce, tomatoes, water, wine, garlic, salt, black pepper, and bell peppers.
3. Bring to a simmer for 30 minutes. Add parmesan cheese and stir.
4. Pour about 1 cup of the sauce on the bottom of 9x13 pan.
5. Arrange 3 uncooked lasagna noodles over sauce, then cover noodles with about 1 cup sauce. Spread 1 cup of the mozzarella cheese over sauce.
6. Repeat layers 2 more times. (noodles, sauce, cheese)
7. Cover with foil and bake for 45 minutes.
8. Remove foil and bake an additional 15 minutes.
9. Let stand 10 minutes before cutting.

Easy Portuguese Chili

It's easily made with the basic ingredients that you'll find in a typical Portuguese home cook's pantry. It's classic comfort food that's hearty and full of flavor. Try this new twist using chouriço. It's an incredible pairing of Mexican and Portuguese flavors.
Serves 8

Ingredients:
1-pound ground beef
1-pound ground chouriço
¼ cup chili powder
1 teaspoon cumin powder
1 teaspoon dried minced onion
1 teaspoon dried minced garlic
1 teaspoon salt
1 ½ teaspoons paprika
Cayenne Pepper (optional) Mild ¼ teaspoon - Medium ½ teaspoon – Hot 1 teaspoon
8 oz. can tomato sauce
8 oz. can of water
1 can of dark kidney beans, with juices
1 can black beans, with juices
Cheddar cheese and green onion for garnish

Directions:
1. Brown ground beef, drain and add to crockpot.
2. Add all other ingredients EXCEPT Cheddar cheese and green onion and mix well.
3. Cover with lid and cook 4 hours on high or 8 hours on low.

Left overs can be frozen and make another meal or quick lunch.

Chouriço Tamale Pie

Every once in a while, you come across a recipe that by adding some Portuguese flavors, it takes it to a new level. What could I possibly not love about a tamale pie baked with a layer of cornbread on top! Cornbread is the perfect accompaniment, which makes this recipe more perfect. Tamale pie with a Portuguese accent. The result is one absolutely phenomenal dinner. Serves 6

Ingredients:
2 tablespoon vegetable oil
1 medium onion finely chopped
1 green bell pepper finely chopped
2 hot peppers seeded and minced (optional)
1-pound ground chouriço
1-pound ground beef
1½ cups frozen corn kernels
1 can (14.5-ounces) diced tomatoes (no need to drain)
3 tablespoons tomato paste
¼ teaspoon garlic powder
½ teaspoon black pepper
1 teaspoon salt
½ cup sliced black olives
4 ounces of 3 or 4 blend Mexican cheese (about 1 cup shredded)
2 boxes of corn muffin mix (like Jiffy)

Directions:
1. Preheat oven to 375 degrees F.
2. In a large skillet over medium heat add the oil. Add the onion and peppers and cook, stirring occasionally, until softened, about 15 minutes. Transfer to a bowl and set aside.
3. On medium heat add the ground beef and chouriço to the pan. Cook, stirring occasionally to break up the ground beef, cook till ground beef no longer pink about 10 minutes.
4. Then add the onion pepper mixture back to the pan. Stir in the corn, diced tomatoes, tomato paste, salt, black pepper and garlic powder. Stir well to ensure that the spices and the tomato paste are evenly distributed. Bring to a simmer, then reduce the heat on low and simmer for 20 minutes. Remove from the heat and let stand while preparing the cornbread topping.
5. Make the Corn mix according to the box directions, set aside.
6. Assemble & Bake the Pie: Stir the olives and shredded cheese into the meat mixture and pour it into a 9x13-inch baking dish, smoothing the top. Pour the cornbread batter over the filling, using a spatula to spread it into an even layer.
7. Bake for 30 to 40 minutes, or until the top is golden brown and a knife inserted into the center comes out clean.
8. Allow the pie to rest for 15 minutes before serving.

Portuguese Stuffed Cabbage Rolls

Stuffed cabbage rolls are the epitome of Polish nourishment. Usually made with ground pork and ground beef mixed with rice are nestled in a cabbage leaf and cooked in the oven or on the stove until tender. This recipe with Portuguese sausage in replace of the ground pork results in a delicious cabbage roll. Even if you're not a fan of cabbage, these stuffed cabbage rolls with a Portuguese accent just might make you a fan! Serves 4

Ingredients:

⅔ cup water
⅓ cup uncooked long grain white rice
8 cabbage leaves
½ pound ground linguiça or chouriço
½ pound ground beef
¼ cup chopped onion
1 egg, slightly beaten
½ teaspoon salt
1 pinch of crushed hot red pepper flakes.
¼ teaspoon ground black pepper
1 (10.75 ounce) can condensed tomato soup

Directions:

1. In a medium saucepan, bring water to a boil. Add rice and stir. Reduce heat, cover and simmer for 20 minutes.
2. Bring a large, wide sauce pan of water to a boil to soften cabbage leaves.
3. Add cabbage leaves and cook for 4 to 5 minutes or until softened; drain.
4. In a medium mixing bowl, combine the ground beef, sausage, 1 cup cooked rice, onion, egg, salt, crushed red pepper and black pepper, along with 2 tablespoons of tomato soup. Mix thoroughly.
5. Divide and add the meat mixture evenly among the cabbage leaves.
6. Roll each one up like you would roll an egg roll wrapper. (roll half way, fold in sides, finish rolling)
7. In a large skillet over medium heat, place the cabbage rolls and pour the remaining tomato soup over the top.
8. Cover and bring to a boil. Reduce heat on low and simmer for about 40 minutes, stirring and basting with the liquid often.

Portuguese Stuffed Peppers

This has been a favorite, and these stuffed peppers with rice, chouriço, and parmesan are one of the most popular recipes on the site, so I don't know why it's taken me so long to feature them again. I'm a long-time fan of stuffed peppers, and I've made a lot of stuffed pepper varieties through the years. What inspired me to create this recipe was having so many fresh bell peppers in my garden. At first, I planned to make a meatless stuffed pepper, but when I found ground chouriço in the fridge, I couldn't resist adding that to the mix. Chouriço and grated parmesan added to the stuffing makes a flavor combination so over-the-top good! Serves 6

Ingredients:

3 green bell peppers
3 red bell peppers
1 tablespoons butter
1 tablespoon olive oil
½ cup chopped onion
1-pound ground linguiça or chouriço
1 ½ cups cooked white rice
1 teaspoon crushed garlic

½ teaspoon dried leaf basil
1 teaspoons salt
½ teaspoon ground black pepper
½ cup grated parmesan cheese
½ cup water
1 can (8 ounces) tomato sauce
Safe top of pepper for baking (optional)

Directions:

1. Cut tops off peppers; remove seeds and membranes, set aside.
2. Heat olive oil and butter in a skillet over medium heat until hot.
3. Sauté chopped onion, for about 10 minutes.
4. In a large mixing bowl add sautéed onion, ground sausage, cooked rice, crushed garlic, basil, salt, pepper, and cheese, mix well.
5. Preheat oven 350 degrees.
6. Add water to a baking dish.
7. Stuff peppers with meat/rice mixture and place snugly in baking dish.
8. Pour tomato mixture over the stuffed peppers.
9. Cover dish tightly with foil and bake for 45 minutes.
10. Remove foil, bake for 15 more minutes.

Peppers should be tender.

Chicken

Portuguese Grilled Chicken page 53

Chicken Madeira

Sautéed chunks of boneless chicken in a savory sauce of mushrooms, garlic, and Madeira wine. Garnish with parsley and serve with white rice or your favorite pasta. Serves 4

Ingredients:
2 pounds boneless, skinless chicken breasts
2 cups Wondra Flour (Cake Flour)
4 teaspoons salt
4 teaspoons oregano
4 tablespoons olive oil
4 tablespoons butter
1 large onion, sliced cut into quarters.
1 teaspoon black pepper
2 packages of sliced mushrooms
1 cup Madeira wine (usually found at your local liquor store)
2 cups chicken broth mixed with 1 teaspoon chopped garlic

Directions:
1. Pound chicken breasts between sheets of "Saran Wrap" until about ¼ inch even-thickness cut into 3-inch pieces.
2. Combine flour, salt, pepper and oregano, blend.
3. Dredge chicken pieces in the flour, shake off excess.
4. Heat oil and butter in frying pan over medium heat. Add onion and sauté for about 5 minutes.
5. Add the dredged chicken and cook the breasts for about four minutes on the first side, until lightly brown.
6. Turn chicken pieces over to second side to cook, add the mushrooms around and on top of the chicken pieces
7. Cook chicken about four more minutes, until lightly browned on the second side, stir the mushrooms.
8. When chicken is browned, add Madeira wine and chicken broth. Mix around the chicken and mushrooms, cover and simmer for about 20 minutes.

Roast Lemon Chicken

I love the smell of a slow roasting chicken in the oven, when you can hear the sizzling of the skin and your whole house smells delicious with the scent of garlic and lemon. This is a simple way to roast chicken, serve it with some mashed potatoes, or rice. Serves 4

Ingredients:
4-6 chicken thighs
1 teaspoon chicken bouillon granules
2 lemons
1 tablespoon minced garlic
2 bay leaves
1 tablespoon olive oil
3 tablespoons butter (cut into small pieces.)

Directions:
1. Place the chicken in a baking dish. Then take the bouillon granules and sprinkle over the chicken.
2. Add the garlic, the juice of the 2 lemons and the bay leaves.
3. Drizzle with olive oil and add the butter on top.
4. Cover with plastic wrap and let sit for about an hour.
5. Remove plastic wrap. Bake in a 375-degree oven for 1 ½ hours or until chicken is cooked and the skin is nice and brown.
6. While cooking, check on it a few times and using a big spoon, scoop up some of the juices and pour over the chicken.

Cranberry Chicken and Rice

Cranberries are just as much a part of the landscape of Cape Cod as sand dunes and beautiful beaches. Cranberry harvests take place throughout the fall. During this time, the bogs on Cape Cod turn into vibrant hosts for wildlife, and sightseers alike. Make this effortless, satisfying, one pot dish that has the bold flavor of cranberries. Celebrate the flavors of fall with chicken cooked in a cranberry sauce. Serves 4

Ingredients:
6 chicken thighs with skin
1 teaspoon salt
¼ teaspoon black pepper
3 medium onions sliced thin
1 cup red wine
1 can gelled cranberries with whole cranberries
2 tablespoons minced garlic
2 tablespoons soy sauce
1 tablespoon dark brown sugar
1 teaspoon white vinegar
¼ teaspoon garlic powder
1 ½ cups chicken stock or chicken broth
1 ½ cups 5-minute white rice

Directions:
1. Preheat oven 375 degrees.
2. Place chicken in a large oven proof casserole and season the chicken with the salt and pepper.
3. Place onions on top of chicken.
4. In a large bowl add all other ingredients, EXCEPT cooked rice, and mix together.
5. Mix till the gelled cranberries are dissolved and pour over chicken and onions.
6. Cook uncovered for 50 minutes.
7. When chicken is done, remove casserole from oven. Let rest for 10 minutes
8. In a sauce pan bring chicken stock to a boil, then add 5-minute rice, stir, and cover and take off heat then let rest for 10 minutes.
9. Serve chicken over rice.

Hot and Spicy Fried Chicken

This crispy fried chicken is inspired by the Portuguese love affair with hot sauce. It was the Portuguese exploration of the African coast, beginning in the 1400s that sparked their huge love affair with the small hot pepper, piri-piri that is an integral part of Portuguese cuisine in several different forms. Unfortunately, it is very difficult to obtain the whole piri-piri pepper in North America. Portuguese specialty shops, which can be found in areas such as New Bedford, MA, where many Portuguese immigrated, will at least carry the bottled sauce. This recipe uses Franks Hot Sauce. Serves 4

Ingredients:
1 cup all-purpose flour
1 cup corn starch
¼ teaspoon dried tarragon
1 tablespoon paprika
½ teaspoon cayenne pepper
3 teaspoons salt
2 teaspoons ground black pepper
1 teaspoon garlic powder
½ teaspoon onion powder

⅓ cup whole milk
¼ cup Franks hot sauce *
1 egg
Legs and chicken thighs (9 pieces)
Oil for deep-fat frying

Brine:
8 cups cold water
¼ cup kosher salt

Directions:
1. Add the chicken pieces to the Brine and refrigerate for an hour.
2. In a shallow bowl, mix the first nine ingredients.
3. In a separate shallow bowl, whisk the milk, hot sauce & egg.
4. Heat the oil on medium high heat to 375° F.
5. Remove chicken from the brine, pat dry to remove any excess liquid.
6. Dip the chicken pieces, one at a time in the flour mixture, then in the milk mixture, then coat again with flour mixture.
7. Put each piece of coated chicken to the side while oil heats.
8. Fry chicken 3 pieces at a time for 9 minutes on each side.

*This Brand of Sauce works great in this recipe.

Portuguese Grilled Chicken

If you've got a little time to factor in the marinating of the chicken (trust me it's worth the effort) this simple dish is well worth the wait. Marinated chicken thighs cooked on the grill basted with a delicious spicy dressing. Serves 4

Ingredients:
4 chicken leg quarters
Juice ½ lemon
3 tablespoons olive oil
½ teaspoon crushed hot red pepper flakes
2 teaspoons minced garlic
1 teaspoon salt

Piri Piri Dressing:
2 tablespoons red wine vinegar
2 tablespoons olive oil
½ teaspoon crushed red hot pepper flakes
2 tablespoons sherry wine
1 tablespoon honey
Make the piri-piri dressing by putting all the ingredients in a screw top jar, shake well.

Directions:
1. Place the lemon juice, oil, salt, hot pepper and garlic in a medium bowl. Whisk to combine.
2. Add the chicken and turn to coat, cover with plastic wrap and marinate in the fridge for about an hour.
3. Pre-heat the grill.
4. Transfer the marinated chicken to the grill. Baste the chicken with the piri piri dressing.
5. Cook the chicken till done.

Piri Piri Grilled Chicken

This Piri Piri Chicken Recipe will add some authentic Portuguese fiery flavor. Its finger licking good! This is a great spicy marinade recipe, great for the Grill. Serves 4

Ingredients:
Zest from 2 lemons and the juice from same 2 lemons
2 red bell peppers seeded and chopped
5 chili peppers like Fresno or Serrano
1 cup fresh parsley leaves
1 tablespoon paprika
1 tablespoon of minced garlic
½ cup red wine vinegar
1 cup olive oil
1 teaspoon salt
½ teaspoons black pepper
Chicken thighs and legs (8 pieces)

Directions:
1. Add all ingredients EXCEPT the chicken to a food processor or blender.
2. Process until it becomes a thick sauce.
3. Reserve ¼ cup of the sauce and set aside for garnishing cooked chicken later.
4. Add chicken pieces in the sauce, refrigerator and let it marinate for at least 1 hour and up to 1 day
5. Place chicken on grill, skin side down first, and grill for about 20 minutes on each side turning occasionally until cooked through.
6. Baste the cooked chicken with the reserved sauce and serve

Roast Chicken with Potatoes and Chouriço

There is nothing better and more comforting than roasted chicken with potatoes and Portuguese sausage. With traditional Portuguese flavors in full swing, these potatoes become tender and delicious. And with the chouriço and chicken on your fork, you end up with magic in your mouth! Serves 6

Ingredients:
6 chicken thighs
5 large red skin potatoes cut into 2-inch chunks
1 link of chouriço, sliced
1 onion chopped
1 ½ teaspoons salt
½ teaspoon ground black pepper
1 teaspoon paprika
1 tablespoon olive oil

Directions:
1. Preheat oven to 375°F.
2. In an oven, safe dish, place the chicken and spread the potatoes, chouriço and onion around chicken, filling the entire dish.
3. Sprinkle evenly over the dish, salt, pepper, and paprika.
4. Drizzle olive oil over dish.
5. Bake, uncovered, for 1 ½ hours. Stir a few times while cooking.

Chicken Curry

This tangy, hot, spicy curry dish has roots by Portuguese colonists. Many of the spices in this dish have roots in Portuguese cuisine. It's derived from the Portuguese dish with "vinha d'alhos" (wine and garlic). This dish was brought to the Goa, India region by Portuguese colonists. Today, this dish is "Indianized" by the local Goan cooks in India, by the substitution of vinegar for the red wine. Many Indian restaurants serve this type of Chicken called "vindaloo". This is a classic dish on the menu. This recipe cooks everything in your crock pot. This recipe is easy and delicious! If you like things Hot and Spicy there won't be any leftovers. Serve with mashed cauliflower, potatoes, or rice.

Ingredients:

2 pounds boneless chicken cut into chunks
1 teaspoon salt
½ teaspoons ground black pepper
1 tablespoon olive oil
1 tablespoon minced garlic
3 onions chopped
1 teaspoon powdered ginger
2 teaspoons cumin powder
2 teaspoons yellow ground mustard
1 teaspoon ground cinnamon

½ teaspoon ground cloves
1 teaspoon turmeric
¼ teaspoon cayenne pepper
1 tablespoon paprika
2 teaspoons lemon juice
¼ cup red port wine
1 tablespoon brown sugar
1 cup tomato sauce
1 cup water

Directions:
Add and mix everything together in crock pot.
Cover with lid and cook 4 hours on high or 8 hours on low.

Seafood

Bacalhau na Brasa page 61

Rhode Island Style Clams

RI Style Clams is a fantastic dish of littleneck clams and chouriço, in a garlicky broth made with white wine, tomato and beans, and every bit sopped up with a crusty bread. A great dish that combines local shellfish with the Italian and Portuguese influences in the area. RI Style Clams is a terrific and easy one to make at home. Serves 4

Ingredients:
2 dozen littleneck clams
2 links chouriço sausage, chopped
1 medium onion peeled and diced
2 teaspoons minced garlic
1 cup diced canned tomatoes, drained
1 15-ounce can white beans
½ teaspoon salt
A pinch of dried thyme
½ cup white wine
½ cup chicken stock
2 tablespoons olive oil
3 tablespoons butter
Bread for serving

Directions:
1. The clams need to be scrubbed under cold running water to remove any sand from the outsides.
2. Add olive oil and butter to a large heavy bottomed pan and sauté 1 onion till soften.
3. Once the onions are soft, add the garlic and chopped links of chouriço sausage and cook along for a few minutes.
4. Then add diced tomatoes and 1 whole, partially drained 15-ounce can of white beans, add thyme, add the littleneck clams, add wine and chicken stock, turn the heat on high and put a lid on top. The clams might not take any more than 5 minutes or so to steam open.
5. Divide the clams into individual bowls and serve them with crusty bread on the side.

Bacalhau Casserole

Portuguese-style cod fish casserole. In Portugal, there are hundreds of ways of cooking cod fish, all of them incredibly tasty! This recipe is no exception. Salt Cod cooked in olive oil, with potatoes, onions, peppers, and garlic. An excellent cod fish dish. Serves 4

Ingredients:

1 ½ pounds dried salted cod. Soak cod in large bowl of water for 30-36 hours in refrigerator with 3 water changes.
5 medium potatoes, peeled, sliced thick
3 eggs, hard-boiled, chopped
1 can large black olives chopped
2 medium onions sliced
½ large red bell pepper, sliced
½ large green bell pepper, sliced
4 teaspoons minced garlic
1 tablespoon hot sauce
3 tablespoons olive oil
½ teaspoon salt
½ teaspoon ground black pepper

Directions:

1. Bring a pot of water to a boil and reduce heat on medium high. Add the soaked salt cod. Boil gently for about fifteen minutes. Drain the fish, but save the water it cooked in. Shred the fish into large chunks, removing any bones and skin and set aside.
2. In the water the Cod cooked in, place the potatoes and bring to a boil. Reduce heat and cook till tender. Drain and set aside.
3. In a skillet, heat olive oil and add the onions, peppers, and garlic. Sauté until vegetables are soft.
4. Mix hot sauce and add salt and pepper. Stir in the cooked codfish and black olives.
5. Pre-heat oven to 375 degrees F.
6. Grease a 2-quart baking dish and layer half of the cooked potatoes along the bottom of the dish.
7. Spread with half the cod and onion mixture. Sprinkle with half of the chopped eggs. Drizzle generously with olive oil. Repeat layers, finishing with another generous drizzle of olive oil.
8. Bake uncovered for about 30 minutes or until the top is golden brown.

Bacalhau na Brasa

I order this at my favorite Portuguese restaurant, O Dinis in East Providence, RI. They grill the fish. This recipe Pan-Seared the fish on a stove top in olive oil. Not surprisingly, this dish has plenty of olive oil. Together with flavorful onions, garlic and "punched potatoes", this is one of those simple combinations of flavors and textures that is characteristically Portuguese. Very easy to make and is delicious! Serves 2

Ingredients:
1 ½ pounds dried salted cod. Soak cod in large bowl of water for 30-36 hours in refrigerator with 3 water changes.
4 new potatoes or red skin
2 tablespoons of melted butter
2 large onions sliced
3 large garlic gloves peeled and sliced
¼ cup extra virgin olive oil and 2 tablespoons, divided
¼ teaspoon salt
¼ teaspoon ground black pepper

Directions:
1. Heat the ¼ cup of olive oil in a large sauté pan over medium heat.
2. Add onions, garlic, salt, and pepper. Cook about 15-20 minutes till onions are soft and translucent. Stir occasionally.
3. Meanwhile; in a small sauce pan add potatoes and cover with water, boil till tender.
4. When onions are cooked, transfer the onions, garlic and olive oil drippings to a bowl, set aside.
5. Add the remaining 2 tablespoons of olive oil to the pan and heat over medium high heat.
6. Drain desalted cod from water and slice into portion sizes.
7. Sear cod in oil for about 5 minutes to brown first side. When you get a nice sear, flip fish over and add the onions and garlic over the top of the pieces of fish with all those delicious oil drippings. Sear second side for about five minutes.
8. Serve fish in serving plates topped with onions and garlic. Add cooked potatoes and punch potatoes down to expose the insides. Drizzle melted butter over potatoes.

Shrimp Mozambique

Despite the African sounding name, this is a Portuguese dish. Mozambique gained their freedom from Portugal in 1975, many of the foods of Mozambique have roots in Portuguese cuisine. Most recipes call for saffron, but sazon goya con azafran makes a great substitute. You can substitute the shrimp for chicken to make it Chicken Mozambique. Serve with cooked white rice.
Serves 4

Ingredients:
3 tablespoons butter
2 medium onions chopped
½ cup white wine
½ cup beer
2 teaspoons Franks Hot Sauce
2 tablespoons minced crushed garlic
1 packet Sazon Goya, for seafood (con azafran)
½ teaspoon salt
½ teaspoon ground black pepper
1 tablespoons chili sauce
1 tablespoon finely chopped fresh cilantro.
12 oz. fresh or frozen medium shrimp peeled and deveined. You can keep the tips on the shrimp, however less messy, especially when you serve over rice.

Directions:
1. Melt butter in large pan over medium heat.
2. Toss in onion and sauté for 15 minutes.
3. Pour in the wine, beer and hot sauce followed by garlic, goya, salt and pepper. Cover and simmer for 8 - 10 minutes, allowing the essence of the spices and herbs to mingle.
4. Mix in chili sauce.
5. Stir. Cover and raise heat to medium-high and bring the sauce to a boil.
6. Toss in the shrimp and cilantro, mix well. Cover and reduce the heat on medium-low and simmer for 10 minutes.
7. Remove from heat and serve with cooked white rice.

Amêijoas 'à bulhão pato'

Clams with lemon and garlic. This Portuguese dish is named after the 19th-century Lisbon poet Bulhão Pato, a well-known gourmand, and today it is a popular first course in many Portuguese restaurants. One thing that Portuguese cuisine does better than the rest, is seafood, especially cooked clams. This is a delicious recipe for one of the most popular Portuguese clam dishes. The buttery and garlicky flavor lends unbelievable taste to this dish that is truly delicious. Serves 4

Ingredients:
2 ¼ pounds little neck clams
6 tablespoons olive oil
4 cloves of garlic sliced
½ teaspoon dry ground coriander
Juice of ½ lemon
½ cup dry white wine
½ teaspoon salt
¼ teaspoon ground black pepper

Directions:
1. Place the clams to soak in water seasoned with 1 teaspoon of salt about 1 to 2 hours. Wash them under running water before cooking.
2. Place the olive oil, and sliced garlic in a skillet and sauté over low heat about 5 minutes.
3. Add the clams, wine, salt, pepper, lemon juice and coriander. Stir, cover the skillet, and cook over medium high heat until the clams open completely. Shake the skillet occasionally.
4. Turn off the heat and serve.

Carne Porco à Alentejana

This is one of the most traditional and popular pork dishes of Portuguese cuisine. Pan seared marinated pork chunks combined with a savory wine sauce. Steamed with little necks and smothered with fried potatoes.
Serves 6

Ingredients:
2 lbs. boneless pork loin cut into 1-inch cubes
2 lbs. potatoes peeled and cut into quarters
2 tablespoons vegetable oil
1 large onion chopped
1 teaspoon sugar
2 tablespoon tomato paste
½ cup of water
24 littleneck clams in the shell, scrubbed
Oil for frying potatoes
black olives and parsley for garnish

Marinade:
1 teaspoon paprika
1 ½ cups dry white wine
¼ teaspoon black pepper
2 teaspoons salt
¼ teaspoon onion powder
1 large bay leaf
3 tsp garlic

Directions:
1. Marinade the pork in a non-metallic bowl in refrigerator overnight.
2. In a large sauce pan, heat oil on medium high heat. Add marinated pork and brown on all sides. Save marinade.
3. Remove pork from pan as you brown meat and set aside.
4. Deglaze pan with the saved marinade and add the sugar and water to the pan and stir.
5. Add chopped onion. Cook about 10 minutes, till onions are translucent.
6. Deep fry or pan fry potatoes at 375 F. degrees for 12 minutes while onions cook. When potatoes are cooked let drain on paper towels or brown paper bag. Shake a little salt and pepper over cooked potatoes while they cool, set aside
7. Add tomato paste to pan, stir and mix well.
8. Add the browned pork back to the pan, stir. Bring pan up to a boil, then add clams on top of the pork, distributing them as evenly as possible. Cover and cook about 20 minutes or until clams open.
9. Add cooked potatoes to pan on top of clam, pork and potatoes and serve.

Amêijoas à Espanhola

There is nothing more delicious than the combination of shellfish and pork. It's a magical pairing. Some food historians think this combination originated with the Spanish Inquisition. It's a fabulous dish, and fun to eat. The double hit of taste from the chouriço and the clams, combined with the peppers and sauce, makes this a classic for a reason.
Serves 6

Ingredients:

24 cherry stone or littleneck clams
1 link of Portuguese chouriço sausage, sliced
2 medium onions sliced
2 tablespoons crushed garlic
1 bay leaf
2 tablespoons olive oil
2 tablespoons butter
2 teaspoons your favorite hot sauce

1 (28 oz.) can crushed tomatoes
4 oz. jar of Goya pimientos sliced
3 peppers, 1 each (green, yellow, orange)
½ cup red wine
1 packet Sazon Goya, for seafood (con azafran)*
1 teaspoon paprika
1 teaspoon salt
½ teaspoon black pepper

Directions:
1. In a large pan, sauté onions in oil and butter over medium heat for 10 minutes.
2. Then add chouriço, peppers and garlic. Cook until peppers are soft.
3. Now add the wine, crushed tomatoes, pimientos and bay leaf. Season with salt, pepper, paprika, hot sauce and Sazon. Let simmer for 20 minutes.
4. Discard bay leaf.
5. Bring to a boil then add littlenecks to the pan cover and cook 10 to 15 minutes or until littlenecks open.

*Sazon Goya, for seafood (con azafran)

Portuguese Mussels

Sweet, plump mussels, at their best are combined with Portuguese sausage in a Portuguese-style stew. After harvesting mussels on the New England coast, Portuguese families would cook them right on the beach in a big pot on a beach grill over hot coals. A Portuguese tradition with this combination of mussels and spicy sausage.

Ingredients:
3 tablespoons olive oil
1 link of chouriço, sliced
1 onion thinly sliced
2 teaspoons minced garlic
1 teaspoon paprika
¼ teaspoon ground black pepper
1 (14.5-oz.) can diced tomatoes, drained
1 cup dry white wine
2 pounds mussels scrubbed

Back-in-the-day Beach Grill

Directions:
1. Heat oil over medium heat.
2. Cook the chouriço and onion for 10 minutes. Stir in the garlic, paprika and pepper.
3. Add the tomatoes. Simmer for 10 minutes.
4. Add wine and the mussels and cover tightly. Increase the heat and cook for 5 minutes, or until the mussels have opened. Discard any mussels that do not open.

Serve with crusty bread, steamed rice or pasta.

Soup - Chowder - Sides

Portuguese Clam Chowder page 71

Portuguese Kale Soup

This recipe for Portuguese kale soup is a crowd favorite that has nourished family and friends for generations. This is a very flavorful soup. The Chouriço gives the broth a good flavor. Kale soup is a winter wonder. Serve with warm crusty bread. A great next day soup and freezes well. Serves 6

Ingredients:

½ gallon of water (8 cups)
4 beef bouillon cubes
1 teaspoon of gravy master or kitchen bouquet
1 bunch of kale. Pull leaves of stems and chop, discard stems
2 links of chouriço, sliced
1 pound of stew meat
½ small head of cabbage, chopped

2 medium onions chopped
½ tablespoon kosher salt
½ teaspoon black pepper
½ cup red wine
¼ teaspoon garlic powder
1 tablespoon olive oil
1 can dark red kidney beans
1-pound potatoes peeled and cut into bite size cubes.

Directions:
1. Bring all ingredients to a boil in at least a 12-quart pot, except potatoes and beans.
2. Cover reduce heat and simmer for 2 hours.
3. Bring back to a boil and add potatoes and beans.
4. Cook till potatoes are done to your liking

Serve with some Portuguese bread or other crusty bread.
Left overs can be frozen and make another meal or quick lunch.

Shrimp Chouriço Corn Chowder

Living in coastal New England, having a good recipe for New England Clam Chowder is an absolute must. You won't go back to clam chowder after this one. It is absolutely delicious! There won't be a drop left in the bowl.

Ingredients:

1 stick salted butter
1 cup ground chouriço
1 small onion diced
2 single stalks celery diced
1 tablespoon minced garlic
½ teaspoon white pepper
½ teaspoon salt
¼ teaspoon hot crushed red pepper
½ cup flour
1 cup clam juice
1 ½ cups chicken broth
1 ¾ cup thawed frozen corn kernels
½ pound raw small shrimp, chopped
¼ cup fresh parsley, chopped
2 cups light cream

Directions:
1. In medium stock pot over medium heat, melt butter and mix in chouriço.
2. Add onions, celery, and garlic and cook over medium heat for 20 minutes.
3. Mix in white pepper, salt and crushed red hot pepper.
4. Mix in flour to make a roux. Cook for 5 minutes over medium low heat.
5. Add clam juice, chicken broth. Mix in well and bring to a simmer, cook for 10 minutes.
6. Add thawed frozen corn kernels, shrimp, and cream. Simmer for 15 minutes and serve.

Portuguese Clam Chowder

In the 1890s, this chowder was called "New York clam chowder" Believe it or not, the addition of tomatoes in place of milk was initially the work of Portuguese immigrants in Rhode Island, as tomato-based stews were already a traditional part of Portuguese cuisine. Since it became so wildly popular, New Englanders then decided to call this modified version "Manhattan-style" clam chowder. Many Portuguese immigrants at that time felt it should have been called, Portuguese Clam Chowder since the Portuguese were the first to create this tomato-based clam chowder.

Ingredients:
1 cup water
¼ cup tomato paste
1 large onion chopped
1 celery stalk chopped
2 tablespoons minced garlic
¼ teaspoon crushed hot red pepper flakes
1 tablespoon kosher salt
½ teaspoon ground black pepper
Pinch dried thyme
1 bay leaf
1 teaspoon dried parsley
2 large potatoes peeled and diced
6 - 8-ounce bottles of clam juice
2 cups of crushed tomatoes
1 ½ cups chopped clams

Directions:
1. Mix tomato paste with water and add to slow cooker with all the other ingredients EXCEPT clams and cook on high for 4 hours.
2. Add clams and cook an additional hour on high.
3. Remove bay leaf and serve.

Portuguese Rice

If you are Portuguese, rice is a staple in your home. Many families grew up having not only Portuguese recipes, but Portuguese rice almost every night of the week. This is a simple and delicious rice dish that is a favorite recipe from Portugal. This is now one of my go-to side dishes! A popular dish full of color and flavor.

Ingredients:
2 tablespoon canola oil
1 cup of uncooked white long grain rice
2 cups water
¼ cup diced green bell pepper
¼ cup diced red bell pepper
½ cup diced onion
1 teaspoon dry chicken bouillon powder
¼ teaspoon ground black pepper
½ teaspoon garlic powder
½ teaspoon paprika
½ teaspoon salt

Directions:
1. Heat oil in a pan over medium heat.
2. Add uncooked dry rice and cook for 5 minutes, stirring occasionally. *
3. Add water, bell peppers, onion, chicken bouillon powder, black pepper, garlic powder, paprika and salt.
4. Cover and simmer for about 20 minutes or till rice is tender, stir occasionally.

*Pan-frying the rice first in oil removes the starchy coating on the rice and makes the rice fluffy instead of sticky. The toasted aroma is wonderful, and you can taste the difference!

Sweets

Lemon Loaf page 78

Malasadas

"Aloha! In Hawaii, malasadas are the ONLY donuts they have! They are sold everywhere in Hawaii. The deep-fried, sugar-dusted fried-dough treat was brought to Hawaii with the 1878 arrival of Portuguese plantation laborers from the Madeira and Azores islands. Malasadas are one of the all-time favorite treats. If you make this, you will rapidly become popular with all your local friends. Makes 1 dozen malasadas. Enjoy!

Ingredients:

3 eggs, room temperature
¾ cup sugar
4 tablespoons unsalted butter, room temperature
¾ teaspoon salt
3¾ cup unbleached all-purpose flour

2 teaspoons yeast
¼ cup warm water
½ cup milk
1 teaspoon vanilla extract
Vegetable oil (for deep-frying)
Additional sugar

Directions:
1. Combine 1 egg, sugar, butter and salt in bowl, beat until blended.
2. Add 3 cups of the flour and yeast, beat 1 minute.
3. Add warm water, milk and vanilla and beat until well blended.
4. Beat in remaining 2 eggs, then ¾ cup flour. Beat until dough is smooth, soft and slightly sticky but begins to come away from sides of bowl, adding more flour by tablespoonful's if very sticky, about 10 minutes. Scrape down dough from sides of bowl.
5. Cover bowl with plastic wrap and towel. Let dough rise in warm draft-free area until almost doubled in volume, about 2 hours.
6. Pour enough oil into large saucepan to reach depth of 1 ½ inches. Attach deep-fry thermometer and heat oil to 350°F.
7. Flour your hands and pull off a piece of dough the size of a lemon. Drop it on a well-floured surface and pat and stretch it into a half-inch thick triangle or square. Fry 2 or 3 malasadas until puffed and golden brown, turning once, about 3 minutes.
8. Using slotted spoon, transfer malasadas to paper towels and drain. Repeat frying with remaining dough, heating oil to 350°F for each batch.
9. Generously sprinkle warm malasadas with additional sugar. Serve warm or at room temperature.

Coconut Cupcakes (Bolinhos de Coco)

The word bolinhos does mean cupcakes, but these aren't, in fact, what most would call a cupcake. This recipe does not include any flour at all (as a matter of fact it's gluten-free). Without flour, it's more like a custard. These are one of the most traditional sweets in Portuguese dessert making. They are a bit size coconut treat. They are simple to make and a great dessert which is sure to impress!

Ingredients:
1 can sweetened condensed milk (14oz can)
2 tablespoons butter
3 eggs
Zest of a half of lemon
½ cup grated sweetened coconut shreds
10 Cupcake Wrappers

Directions:
1. Preheat the oven to 350 F.
2. Add the cupcake wrappers to muffin pan.
3. Place all the ingredients in a bowl and beat on high for 30 seconds.
4. Pour the batter almost to the top of each wrapper.
5. Sprinkle a little shredded coconut on top of batter.
6. Bake for about 30 minutes until the tops have browned a bit.
7. Remove from oven and allow to cool.

The muffins will be plump when you first take them out of the oven, but will sink as they cool. This is perfectly normal.

Pumpkin Dreams

I love pumpkin dreams all year long. Moist and delicious every time. Everyone asks for the recipe after they've tried them!

Ingredients:
1¾ cups all-purpose flour
2 teaspoons baking powder
½ teaspoon salt
½ teaspoon cinnamon
½ teaspoon nutmeg
½ teaspoon allspice
⅛ teaspoon ground cloves
⅓ cup vegetable oil
½ cup brown sugar
1 egg
1 teaspoon vanilla extract
¾ cup canned pumpkin
½ cup milk

Coating
1 stick unsalted butter, melted
2/3 cup sugar
2 tablespoons cinnamon

Directions:
1. Preheat oven to 350 F and spray mini muffin tins with non-stick cooking spray.
2. Combine flour, baking powder, salt, and spices in a bowl and whisk until combine.
3. In another bowl, mix oil, brown sugar, egg, vanilla, pumpkin, and milk.
4. Pour in flour mixture into the wet and mix until just combined.
5. Fill mini muffin tins until almost full and bake 10-12 minutes. Let cool
6. Melt butter in small bowl.
7. Mix sugar and cinnamon in a separate small bowl.
8. After pumpkin dreams, have cooled for a few minutes, dip them in the butter and roll them in the sugar mixture.

Lemon Loaf

You will love this moist, delicious Lemon cake! This easy to make recipe is loaded with delicious lemon flavor and topped with an amazing lemon frosting. There is something about that delicious, moist cake that keeps us all coming back for more. Its rich, moist, perfectly flavored lemon cake topped with the perfect layer of lemon frosting.

Ingredients:

1 ½ cup flour
½ teaspoon baking soda
½ teaspoon baking powder
½ teaspoon salt
3 eggs
1 cup sugar

2 tablespoons butter, softened.
1 teaspoon vanilla extract
1 teaspoon lemon extract
⅓ cup lemon juice
½ cup oil (recommend coconut oil)

Lemon Icing

1 cup powdered sugar; plus 1 tablespoon.
2 tablespoons whole milk
½ teaspoon lemon extract

Directions:

1. Combine flour, baking soda, baking powder and salt in a bowl, set aside.
2. Use a mixer to blend together the eggs, sugar, butter, vanilla, lemon extract, lemon juice and oil in a medium bowl.
3. With mixer on, pour dry ingredient into the wet ingredients and blend until smooth.
4. Pour batter into a well-greased 9x5-inch loaf pan.
5. Bake at 350 degrees for 45 minutes or until a toothpick stuck into center of the cake comes out clean.
6. Make the lemon icing by combining all the icing ingredients in a small bowl with an electric mixer on low speed.
7. When the loaf is cool, remove it from pan and frost the top with the icing.
8. Let the icing set up before slicing.

Coconut Cake (Bolo de Coco)

This cake is moist and delicious! Irresistible best describes this cake. You will want to eat several pieces! Brazilians absolutely love cakes. They like a simple cake that they can eat for breakfast that will have tons of flavor and just hit the spot to start the day right. This recipe comes from Brazil. It is out of this world – a coconut lover's dream.

Ingredients:
3 eggs
2 cups of sugar
3 tablespoons unsalted butter
1 cup milk
1 teaspoon vanilla extract
½ teaspoon almond extract
Zest from ½ lemon
3 cups of flour
1 tablespoons of baking powder
¼ teaspoon salt

Topping:
1 can sweetened condensed milk
1 can coconut milk Use about 13.5 fl oz. (unsweetened)
Grated coconut to sprinkle (sweetened or unsweetened)

Directions:
1. Pre-heat oven to 350 F. degrees
2. In a bowl beat together the eggs, sugar and butter then gradually add milk, vanilla, almond and zest.
3. In a separate bowl mix, together flour, baking powder and salt.
4. Gradually add flour to bowl of wet ingredients and mix together.
5. Grease a 10 x 7 pan and dust with flour and then pour batter into pan.
6. Bake for about 30 min or until lightly browned.
7. While the cake is baking, make the topping by mixing both milk ingredients together and set aside.
8. When cake is done, remove the cake from the oven and while still warm spread topping all over top of cake.
9. Sprinkle grated coconut all over the top and allow to cool.

Pasteis de Nata (Custard Tarts)

A traditional Portuguese pastry. Pastéis de nata were created before the 18th century by Catholic monks at the Jerónimos Monastery in the civil parish of Santa Maria de Belém, in Lisbon. These monks were originally based in France and loved these pastries which could be found in local French bakeries. At the time, convents and monasteries used large quantities of egg-whites for starching of clothes, such as nuns' habits. It was quite common for monasteries and convents to use the leftover egg yolks to make cakes and pastries, resulting in this sweet pastry recipes throughout the country. Makes 24 Custard Tarts

For the dough:
1 box frozen Pepperidge Farm Puff Pastry Sheets
1 Wide Mouth Quart Mason Jar
2 -12 cup muffin pans

For the custard:
3 tablespoons white corn flour*
1 ¼ cups milk, divided
1 ⅓ cups granulated sugar
2/3 cup water
2 cinnamon sticks
Whole peel of 1 lemon, divided
½ teaspoon vanilla extract
6 large egg yolks

For the garnish
Confectioners' sugar

Directions for the Dough:
1. Grease muffin pan.
2. Place one unfolded sheet of pastry on a lightly floured surface.
3. Take a wide mouth "Ball" mason jar. Turn upside down and press the glass top into the dough to cut out 12 circular pieces of dough. You will get about 9 and should combine the left-over pieces of dough and roll out to get 3 more pieces.
4. Repeat with 2nd pastry sheet.

Directions for the Custard:
1. Pre-heat oven to 475 degrees F.
2. In a medium bowl, whisk the flour and ¼ cup milk until smooth, set aside.
3. In a small sauce pan bring the sugar, half of the lemon peel, 1 cinnamon stick, and water to a boil. Over medium heat cook until sugar dissolves in the water. Don't overcook, liquid should still be clear when sugar is dissolved.
4. Meanwhile, in another small saucepan, add the remaining 1 cup milk with the remaining lemon peel and cinnamon stick. Once milk begins to boil, remove from heat.
5. Remove the lemon peel and cinnamon stick and whisk the hot milk into the flour/milk mixture you set aside earlier.
6. Remove the lemon peel and cinnamon stick from the sugar syrup and then pour the sugar syrup into the hot milk-and-flour mixture, whisking briskly. Add the vanilla and stir for about a minute.
7. Whisk in the yolks, one at a time. (You can refrigerate the custard for up to 3 days.)
8. Take out the 12 cup muffin pans.
9. Pour the custard 3 quarters of the way up into each pastry shell.
10. On bottom rack bake for 20 minutes.
11. A proper pastel has those little brown spots on top. If the pastéis don't have them but are fully baked, you can then put them under the broiler for a few minutes that should do the trick.
12. Cool and garnish with Confectioners' sugar.

Easy Apple Tart

This Easy Apple Tart has structure and a delicious taste! Tarte de Maçã, or Portuguese Apple Tart, is a signature of Portuguese dessert making. It combines fresh apples with a flaky crust and a slightly citrus lemon twist.

Ingredients:
1 sheet (½ package) Pepperidge Farm Puff Pastry
2 large apples (cored, halved and sliced into very thin slices)
Juice of ½ lemon (about 1 tablespoon)
½ cup brown sugar
½ cup regular sugar
½ teaspoon cinnamon
¼ teaspoon salt
Powdered sugar

Directions:
1. Preheat oven to 400 F.
2. Thaw puff pastry at room temperature about 45 minutes (per package directions).
3. On a lightly floured surface, unfold one sheet of pastry. Cut the pastry in half, creating two rectangles.
4. Place one of the dough rectangles on a baking sheet lined with parchment paper or sprayed lightly with cooking spray.
5. In a small bowl, combine brown and regular sugar, cinnamon and salt.
6. Put apple slices to a large bowl and squeeze the juice from ½ of a lemon onto apples. Stir to coat.
7. Then, add the contents of the cinnamon and sugar bowl to the apples. Stir to coat.
8. Arrange apple slices on puff pastry dough (like shingles), leaving about ¼ inch of dough exposed on all sides.
9. Add the other half of the dough on top of the apples and pinch the dough together to the bottom dough around all edges.
10. Cut slices down the top of the dough about an inch apart.
11. Bake in preheated oven for 20 minutes

Sprinkle with sifted powdered sugar, as desired.

Portuguese Rice Pudding (Arroz Doce)

Portuguese rice pudding, or Arroz Doce, is one of the most popular and traditional desserts in Portuguese cuisine. It is a unique dish with simple ingredients which are combined to create a deliciously sweet and creamy egg-based rice pudding.

Ingredients:
2 cups water
Lemon peel of 1 whole lemon
2 cinnamon sticks
¼ teaspoon salt
1 cup short grain rice (or medium grain rice)
2 ½ cups hot milk
2 ½ cups half-and-half
⅔ cup sugar
3 egg yolks
Cinnamon for garnish

Directions:
1. In a saucepan add the water, lemon peel, cinnamon sticks, and salt, bring to a boil.
2. While it's boiling, add the rice.
3. Reduce the heat and simmer for 15 minutes or until almost all the water has been absorbed.
4. Add the milk, half-and-half and sugar to the rice.
5. Increase the heat to medium-high and bring to a simmer, then reduce the heat to maintain a simmer. Cook, uncovered, and stirring frequently, until the mixture starts to thicken, about 30 minutes.
6. In a separate bowl, beat the egg yolks together. Add 3 tablespoons of the rice mixture one tablespoon at a time to temper the eggs. Make sure you are beating the eggs vigorously while adding the 3 tablespoons of the rice mixture.
7. Now add that egg mixture quickly into the saucepan.
8. Let the rice continue to simmer for about 10 minutes to allow the rice to thicken. It should form a nice creamy consistency.
9. Remove lemon peel and cinnamon sticks.
10. Transfer to one large serving dish or small dessert cups.

Garnish with cinnamon.

Made in the USA
San Bernardino, CA
01 December 2019